Zodiac Coloring Book.

ARIES

Fire Sign

Honest, Confident & Passionate.

TAURUS

Earth Sign
Reliable, Devoted & Stubborn.

Stubborn

Reliable

Devoted

GEMINI

Air Sign

Impulsive, Adaptable & Outgoing.

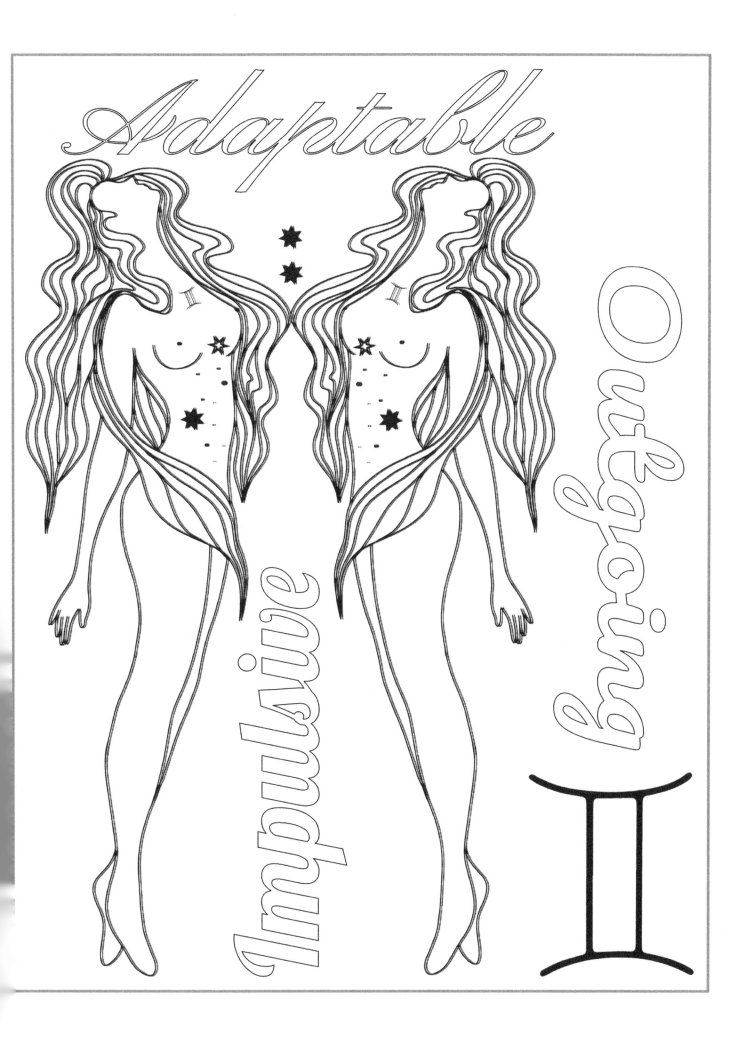

CANCER

Water Sign

Caring, Loyal & Protective.

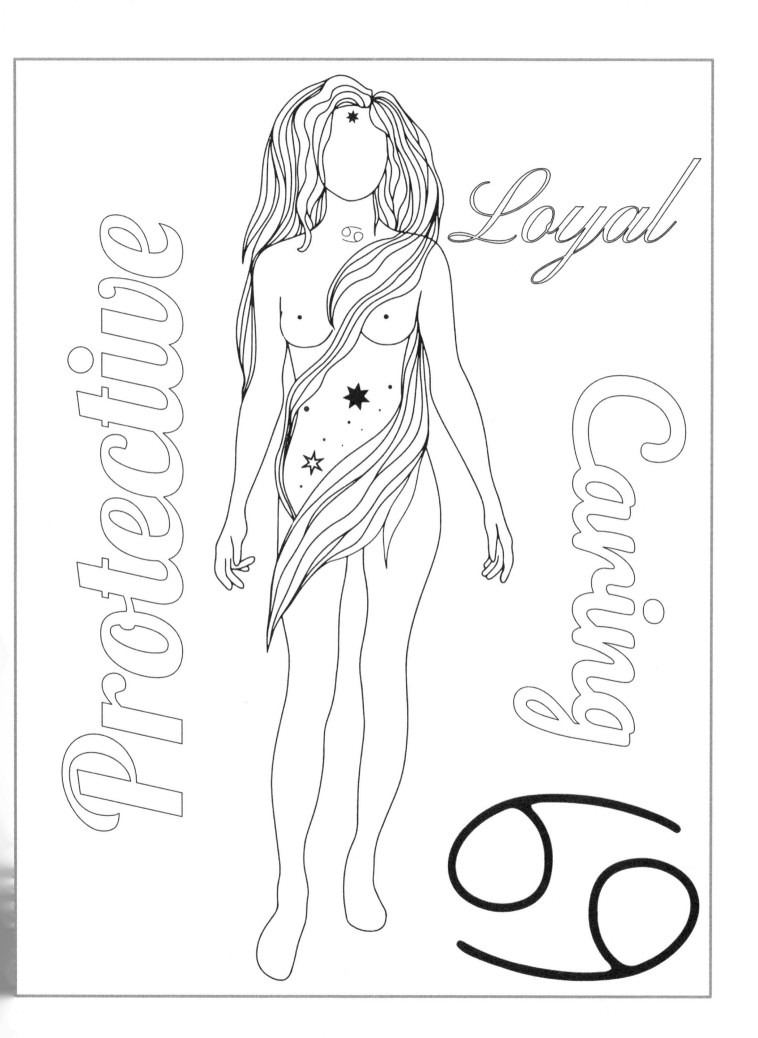

LEO

Fire Sign

Popular, Warm & Passionate.

VIRGO

Earth Sign

Intense, Observant & Strong.

LIBRA

Air Sign

Diplomatic, Social & Clever.

SCORPIO

Water Sign

Brave, Honest & Ambitious.

SAGITTARIUS

Fire Sign

Fun, Restless & Fair Minded.

CAPRICORN

Earth Sign

Realistic, Practical & Disciplined.

AQUARIUS

Air Sign

Assertive, Original & Independant.

PISCES

Water Sign

Imaginative, Mystical & Artistic.

Imaginative

Mystical

Artistic ♓